THE
*Archive Photographs*
SERIES

# MILES AIRCRAFT

The name behind the company – Frederick George Miles, seen here in a happy moment at Woodley, probably in the days immediately before the outbreak of war. He was seldom referred to by his christian name; for the most part he was known as Miles. His restless energy was the driving force behind the extraordinary variety of projects and products produced by Phillips & Powis and Miles Aircraft during their relatively short history.

THE
*Archive Photographs*
SERIES

# MILES AIRCRAFT

*Compiled by*
Rod Simpson

**CHALFORD**

The Chalford Publishing Company
St Mary's Mill, Chalford,
Stroud, Gloucestershire, GL6 8NX

ISBN 0 7524 1091 1

Typesetting and origination by
The Chalford Publishing Company
Printed in Great Britain by
Bailey Print, Dursley, Gloucestershire

Miles M.2P Hawk Major, G-ADLO is seen over Woodley prior to its delivery to New Zealand in 1937.

# Contents

| | | |
|---|---|---|
| | Acknowledgements | 6 |
| | Introduction | 7 |
| 1. | In the Beginning | 15 |
| 2. | Racing and Touring | 27 |
| 3. | Training for War | 53 |
| 4. | Research and Development | 95 |
| 5 | Planes for Peace | 107 |

# Acknowledgements

Few books are successful just because of the skill of the author and the Chalford Archive Photographs Series has gained its reputation as a result of the work of photographers and the variety of pictures included in the individual volumes. In preparing this book on Miles Aircraft I am very grateful to a number of friends who have enthusiastically helped with information, and with their own photographs and those they have collected.

Above all, I must thank The Adwest Group plc and its Chief Executive, Graham Menzies, for access to their historical archive. Under the watchful eye of Julian Temple, this unique material has been kept safe since its recovery from near disaster in 1967. Many companies have little regard for their history and Adwest are to be congratulated on taking such care to preserve these records. Julian Temple has also been a source of great support and his excellent book, *Wings over Woodley* has provided much detail for the text supporting the photographs.

I am also most grateful to Peter Amos for providing so much help with the detailed history. Peter has spent a lifetime researching Miles and not only continues to turn up snippets which add vital pieces to the jigsaw, but also devotes heart and soul to The Miles Aircraft Collection and its publication *The Miles Magazine*. The Museum of Berkshire Aviation, which preserves many Miles artifacts, has also been of great assistance, as has Jim Halley who provided many of the individual histories of military Miles aircraft.

Many photos have also been lent by fellow historians and members of Air-Britain, particularly Michael Stroud, John Havers and Mike Hooks, who has pulled many rare shots from his mysterious photo boxes. If I have left anyone out, then I apologise, but the individual pictures provided for the book, other than those from my own collection are as follows. They are identified by page number with T indicating the top picture and B, the bottom:
Adwest Group/Julian Temple: Cover, 2, 9T, 9B, 11, 12, 13, 22T, 54T, 55T, 87T, 87B, 94, 96T, 96B, 102T, 106, 109B. Mike Hooks: 17B, 20B, 33B, 34T, 34B, 35T, 51B, 55B, 68T, 77T, 111T, 112B, 113T, 113B, 116B, 121B, 122B, 126T, 126B, 127T, 128T. John Havers: 17T. Peter Amos: 41T, 45B, 52, 59B, 60, 69, 81T, 96B, 128B.

Rod Simpson, 1998

# Introduction

One of the most vibrant British aircraft companies of all time was born in 1932, lived for fifteen years and collapsed in September 1947. The creators of this remarkable business were Frederick George Miles and his brother George. 'Miles', as F.G. Miles was universally known, was the one with drive, enthusiasm and extraordinary vision in aircraft design. His brother was the more thoughtful and, in many ways, the more stable and creative of the pair. Between them they developed a range of aircraft which led the world.

Following the end of the First World War, with the support of his father, owner of a Portslade laundry business, the young F.G. Miles was able to channel his enthusiasm for aviation into barnstorming and joyriding with Avro 504s, the development of a flying school helped by the legendary Cecil Pashley and aircraft manufacture. Miles' first design, the Gnat biplane, served as a useful learning experience but in 1929 Southern Aircraft Ltd was formed at Shoreham to build the Martlet single-seater. Based on the Avro Baby, the Martlet was quite successful and six examples, together with a single Metal Martlet, were completed.

At this stage, Miles detached himself from the growing flying school and aircraft maintenance business, leaving brother George to manage its development. A major reason for the change of direction was F.G.'s marriage to 'Blossom', the former wife of one of the other directors of Southern Aircraft and herself, the acquiror of one of the production Southern Martlets. Together they moved to Sevenoaks and there designed another light aircraft, the Satyr. Blossom showed great flair for practical aircraft design and draftmanship which paid dividends in future years and the single example of the Satyr exhibited the excellent flying characteristics which stayed with all future Miles aircraft.

For some while, Miles had been doing business with Charles Powis, a Reading garage owner and operator of Phillips & Powis Aircraft. In 1932, Miles was encouraged to move to Reading and work on the concept they had jointly developed for a new light aircraft. It would bring modern affordable training to flying clubs which were operating largely with de Havilland Moths of various types. The Miles Hawk was an all-wood low-wing monoplane with two seats and wings which could be folded for easy storage. In this endeavour, Miles was supported by Blossom and by the engineer, Harry Hull, who followed him from the days at Shoreham. The Hawk was an excellent performer and quickly gained acclaim – and orders. It started a Miles tradition of taking part in the air races which were all the rage in the early 1930s and brought home significant prizes. Phillips & Powis was becoming a talking point in aviation circles and by the spring of 1934 was building one aircraft a week.

Light aircraft of this era were similar to quality motor cars; they were largely hand-built and invariably modified to the specific needs of the customer. Various customised flavours of Hawk emerged from the Woodley factory. Special Hawks were created for long range flights to South Africa and other parts of the world and the 'standard' Hawk progressed to become the Hawk Major which used a Gipsy Major engine in place of the original Cirrus. Further success came in the 1934 King's Cup Air Race with Flight Lieutenant Tommy Rose achieving second place in an M.2P Hawk Major. Miles also built three examples of the Hawk Speed Six which were specialised air racers – and, for the 1935 King's Cup, the M.5 Sparrowhawk which was designed to F.G. Miles' precise instructions and had a maximum speed of 178 mph using a 140 hp Gipsy Major engine.

It was not long before the Miles product range widened to include a three/four seat cabin tourer. The M.3A Falcon Major and the later M.3B Falcon Six brought comfortable high speed transport to private owners and, again, Tommy Rose used a Falcon as his mount to win the 1935 Kings Cup. A total of 36 examples was completed. Miles later built 50 of the two-seat Whitney Straight club trainer which followed similar design lines.

By 1935, the first ripples of preparation for war were being seen. Miles started to equip the Reserve Flying Training Schools with Hawk Trainers and the airfield at Woodley saw the establishment of No. 8 ERFTS and expansion of the Phillips & Powis factory buildings. Phillips & Powis received orders for several batches of the military M.14 Magister which equipped RAF flying training schools. Magisters were exported to Eire and Egypt from these RAF batches and a licence was granted for production of the M.14 in Turkey, although it is thought that none were actually built there. After the war, the Magister was civilianised in large numbers and equipped many flying clubs and schools under the name Hawk Trainer III.

At about this time, Miles realised that the training programme for the new Hurricanes and Spitfires needed something more sophisticated than Hawk Trainers and Tiger Moths and he designed a tandem two-seat Private Venture trainer designated M.9. The M.9 later adopted the name Kestrel from the Rolls Royce Kestrel engine which was installed. This may also have had something to do with the fact that Rolls Royce provided the engine and eventually became a major investor in Phillips & Powis! This took Miles into negotiations with the Air Ministry (and subsequently the Ministry of Aircraft Production) which were to become frequently frustrating, occasionally rewarding and sometimes stormy for the go-ahead young entrepreneur.

Fortunately, in June 1938, after some prevarication, the Ministry placed a large £2 million order for the production M.9 Master I. This aircraft closely followed the design of the Kestrel but problems arising from the weight and balance calculations resulted in its being fitted with a belly-mounted radiator rather than the chin-mounted unit of the original prototype. Masters started reaching 8 FTS in the late summer of 1939 where they were a key factor in preparation of aircrew for the Battle of Britain. The company rapidly changed from a largely hand-built process to a modern moving production line

Woodley was a busy place in 1938. This view of the Repair and Service Department hangar shows new production Whitney Straights awaiting delivery and the Tiger Moths of the Reserve Flying Training school in the background. A lone BA Swallow awaiting repair is an interloper among this Miles-dominated group.

Quiet inspiration for Miles came from the remarkable 'Blossom'. The former Maxine Freeman-Thomas married 'Miles' in August 1932 and applied her talents to aircraft design, development of the training programme and much more. Blossom and Miles had two children – Jeremy and Mary. Here, Blossom is seen with Mary in a quiet moment at the family home.

which was vital to meet the wartime demand for Masters. What is more, the Master was a much more complex aircraft than the Hawk Trainer and Whitney Straight so the workforce at Woodley had to be expanded and trained to produce the thirty aircraft per month required by the production schedule. Amazingly, 500 Masters had been completed by September 1940, and Phillips & Powis had also been able to expand all its administrative services to cope with the considerable challenge posed by wartime pressures. It was the need for a skilled factory workforce which prompted Miles to establish the Miles Aeronautical Technical School in March 1943. This was a special project of Blossom Miles and, aimed at training junior draftsmen and technicians including theoretical instruction in aerodynamics, mathematics, aircraft materials and drawing office procedure.

The Master I led to further variants. The Master II and Master III were the same airframe fitted with Bristol Mercury and Pratt & Whitney Wasp Junior radial engines respectively. Miles had the bright idea of producing a Master Fighter – essentially a Master I with a single-seat cockpit and six Browning .303 machine guns. Some 24 examples of this were completed and put into service with the Flying Training Schools for advanced fighter training. Miles was also concerned that production of front line fighter types such as the Spitfire was expensive and labour intensive and he felt that there was a pressing need for a fighter which could be built quickly and in very large numbers. To this end, the company designed, built and flew the prototype M.20 fighter which was based on a project produced as a mock-up by the company just before the war. It had some features of the Master and, despite having a fixed undercarriage was faster than the Hawker Hurricane. If the Battle of Britain had turned out differently, the M.20 might have had its day but in the event only two examples were completed.

Throughout the war the inventive brain of Miles came up with projects to meet almost every requirement of the RAF. There were the M.21 and Marlborough crew trainer projects, a high-speed twin-engined fighter, the M.22, and the Rolls Royce Griffon engined M.23 Spitfire lookalike. Most of these projects failed to capture the limited imagination of the Air Ministry but Miles did build large numbers of the Martinet target tug derived from the Master and received an order for the M.33 Monitor twin-engined target tug. The construction of the Monitor broke with Miles tradition in having an all-metal fuselage matched to the wooden wings which were more familiar to the Miles workforce. However, the war was nearing a close and the original order for 600 aircraft was progressively cut back until production was halted with only 20 aircraft completed.

Miles experimented with many other ideas. Designs were produced for numerous trainers at the small Research and Development Department set up in a former biscuit tin factory at Liverpool Road, Reading. They built the M.35 Libellula and the later M.39 to test the concept of tail-first bomber and naval fighter designs and in their spare time the Liverpool Road staff designed and built a low-wing civil two-seater designated LR.5 and nicknamed *The Bolshie*. The company also invented numerous aircraft systems which were to become profitable products in their own right. Notable were the Miles Co-Pilot lightweight aircraft autopilot and the Miles actuator, which became widely used to operate all types of moving components of aircraft and other machines.

In 1943, the name Phillips & Powis was changed to Miles Aircraft Ltd following F.G. Miles' acquisition of the Rolls Royce interest in the company. Miles had always been fascinated by the possibilities of large transport aircraft and realised that long-

By the autumn of 1938 the Phillips & Powis factory at Woodley had grown far beyond its original layout and preparations for war were a major preoccupation. This picture, taken at the time of the Munich Crisis, shows the much-expanded factory with a new flight shed, assembly section, dope shop and metalworking section. To the north of the main complex is the original Phillips & Powis repair and service hangar. The empty area between the two groups of buildings is what remains of the Reserve Flying Training School which burned down in October 1938. In the bottom centre is the newly-constructed rifle range and the work in hand on construction of air raid shelters is clear on the lower right hand side. The Falcon Hotel, a famous Woodley landmark, is towards the top right.

range travel by air would be a major growth area in the post-war world. He had devised the 'X' designs in the 1930s covering a range of radically different airliners and these were revived for presentation to the Ministry. The principle of the 'X' design was a smoothly flowing join of wing and fuselage which would allow the aircraft to have an exceptionally wide and comfortable passenger cabin. The 'X' fuselage would be an aerofoil section providing its own lift and the engines would be buried in the wings so as to minimise drag. In characteristic fashion, the Miles brothers decided that the only way to test the theory was to build what would today be called a 'proof of concept' prototype. The Miles X-Minor was constructed and flown but, in the end the 'X' principle was not applied to a production airliner and the Americans came to dominate the long-range transport scene after the war.

Miles and Blossom had all the confidence which the thirties brought – and their home reflected their modern, progressive attitudes. Lands End House, designed by Guy Morgan, was completed in 1934 and was 'state of the art'. By the time this picture was taken, the war had arrived and the house was camouflaged – and the front doorway was adorned with a cartoon of Hitler getting 'the order of the boot'!

The most ambitious research project, however, was the M.52. It was, perhaps, surprising that the Ministry should accept this proposal for a supersonic jet research aircraft, but a contract was awarded and the Miles team designed a small aircraft with a cylindrical fuselage just large enough to contain the jet engine and very thin wings with a biconvex aerofoil section. This wing was tested on a Falcon light aircraft which became known as the 'Gillette Falcon' by virtue of the very sharp wing leading edge. Models of the M.52 were tested in the Miles wind tunnel and a full-size mock-up was constructed. Parts for the first prototype were under construction in February 1946 when the Ministry of Supply summarily cancelled the project. The technical data was then handed over to the US Government and emerged in the design of the Bell X-1. This episode was, sadly, an early example of the frustrated decisions which dogged British advanced aviation projects for the next two decades.

The arrival of peace brought other pressures for Miles Aircraft. Like all other wartime armament companies, they had expanded their facilities and workforce to meet the huge demand but, in 1945, the bulk of outstanding orders were cancelled. Fortunately, they had designed the Miles Messenger liaison aircraft which was delivered in small numbers to the RAF and was used, particularly, by Field Marshall Bernard Montgomery. The Messenger went into production at the Miles factory in Northern Ireland for civil customers and was joined by its twin-engined version, the M.65 Gemini. The Gemini shared production space at Woodley with the Aerovan light freighter, which sold to the various small transport companies which blossomed after the war in the hands of ex-RAF pilots. Miles benefited from the desire of returning aircrew to stay in the air and a satisfactory volume of orders flowed in to the Woodley sales office.

The post-war Miles factory was a hive of activity. The experimental M.71 Merchantman which was, essentially, a scaled-up four-engined Aerovan, flew in August 1947, as did the M.68 Boxcar, which incorporated a removable freight container which fitted under the centre fuselage. Miles expanded into other non-aviation products including the Copycat, which was one of the earliest photocopiers, and launched the famous Biro ballpoint pen. Workers in the pen factory on the opposite side of the road from the main plant could be found with microscopes inserting the tiny ballbearing into the tip of the Biro pen core! Without doubt, the major expansion project was the Miles M.60 Marathon transport which would finally take the company out of its traditional wooden airframes into all-metal construction. Two Marathon prototypes had flown by February 1947 and prospects of orders from BOAC and BEA were strong, even though the company had to battle with the customary bureaucratic indecision.

Unfortunately, all this peacetime development brought its burdens. Financially, Miles Aircraft Ltd had to cope with the manufacturing startup costs of all its new production aircraft and the investment in the Marathon, Merchantman and Boxcar. The Messenger, Gemini and Aerovan were selling below the cost of production – although that situation was gradually being overcome. The post-war profits tax regime was also penalising the company. By the end of 1946, plans were afoot to raise additional capital, but the terrible winter and fuel shortages of early 1947 brought

George Miles brought the vision of F.G. Miles to reality. Here he is seen in 1944 holding a model of the proposed jet-engined M.63 Libellula Mailplane.

The Miles Aerovan was seen as an all-purpose flying truck. In one experiment G-AILF was used to test techniques for planting crops from the air and is seen here sitting in a muddy field in Northamptonshire.

chaos to the Woodley factory. Glued joints would not set in the extreme cold, supplies of components were held up and deliveries of new aircraft to customers slowed to a trickle. In September 1947 the company's auditor, Samuel Hogg, presented a report which painted such a pessimistic view of Miles Aircraft's viability that the banks withdrew further financial support. In November, Samuel Hogg was appointed Receiver and this was followed, in due course, by the departure of the Miles brothers. The once-proud Miles Aircraft ceased all aircraft production. It was a victim of post-war recession, the indifference of bureaucrats who have secure salaries and are blind to the commercial realities of business, and the sad truth that accountants will often find a way of triumphing over visionaries.

From this spectacular collapse emerged a new order. Handley Page took over the Marathon programme and the main Miles aviation assets, and the Western Manufacturing Company was formed to develop the general engineering skills of the business. Today, its successor, Adwest Group plc, forges ahead with the high quality tradition established by Miles Aircraft. As for F.G. Miles, he re-established the Miles name at Redhill in 1948 and moved on to Shoreham in 1953 where he was rejoined by George Miles. Their company, F.G. Miles Ltd, merged with Auster Aircraft in October 1960 to form the new Beagle Aircraft, and the design influence of George Miles was seen in the Beagle 218 light twin and the Beagle Pup. George Miles later set up a new company at Ford to carry out aircraft engineering and develop new designs. The aircraft which were built by Miles Aircraft have an enduring quality. Today, many Miles aircraft still fly and the surviving examples, some of which are illustrated in this archive collection, are much loved and cherished by their proud owners.

# One

# In the Beginning

*For F.G. Miles the very early days were spent on various engineering projects including designing and building a motor car – but the aviation bug soon caught hold of him. Miles' flying school and barnstorming activities led to the establishment of the aerodrome at Shoreham and to the design and production of a small series of Southern Martlet biplanes. After these small beginnings the opportunity to join Charles Powis and to conceive and build a new light aircraft was irresistable. Powis had started in the motorcycle repair business with Jack Phillips but branched out into aviation and established Reading Aerodrome at Woodley, with a flying school and 'aviation service station'. With the aviation expertise of Miles and financial backing from Powis, the business was to develop into a major aircraft manufacturer.*

*Having moved to Woodley near Reading, Miles, now aged 30, designed the Hawk, which quickly became a success due to its simple construction, ease of maintenance and good flying manners. These were the glorious days in the 1930s when a small company such as Phillips & Powis was able to produce aircraft rapidly and had to cope with less stringent certification requirements than those which later burdened aircraft manufacturers. The confidence of F.G. Miles led to the production of many new variants of the open two-seat Hawk monoplane which were destined to establish a powerful and unique place for British light aircraft.*

Southern Aircraft's hangars at Shoreham provide the backdrop for the prototype Metal Martlet, G-ABJW (incorrectly painted as G-AAJW) on the right, and one of the six Southern Martlets which were built between 1929 and 1931.

Most production Martlets used the 85 hp Armstrong Siddeley Genet II five-cylinder radial engine but the fourth Martlet, G-AAYX, was built as an aerobatic aircraft with a 105 hp Genet Major. Surviving the war, it passed to Billy Butlin of holiday camp fame, and then reached the Shuttleworth Collection at Old Warden where it is currently under restoration.

The tiny single-seat M.1 Satyr was the first design of the independent F.G. Miles following his departure from Southern Aircraft and was designed by Miles and Blossom from their Sevenoaks flat. The sole prototype, G-ABVG, was first flown from Yate by Miles on 31 July 1932, powered by a 75 hp Pobjoy R radial engine.

The Satyr was a popular air show performer and is seen here sitting beneath a Rollason Air Services DH.89, painted in the distinctive checkerboard colour scheme applied for the barnstorming activities. It was substantially damaged in 1936 when Mrs Victor Bruce flew into telephone cables while landing in a farmer's field.

Charles Powis and F.G. Miles conceived a new low-cost light aircraft which was named the Hawk. Unusually for its time, the Hawk had a low wing layout. The first M.2 Hawk flew on 29 March 1933 and was followed by a substantial production run commencing with G-ACHJ, which is shown here at the 1933 King's Cup Air Race.

The Hawk, G-ACYA was typical of the breed with its 95 hp Cirrus III engine of which a plentiful stock was available to Phillips & Powis Aircraft. This Hawk was delivered to F.D. Bradbrooke in August 1933 and ended its life in a hangar fire at Hooton seven years later.

The first major variation on the Hawk theme was the three-seat M.2D, of which six were built. It had increased span wings and an enlarged rear cockpit for two passengers seated in tandem. The prototype M.2D, which had an operational life of only three years, carried the temporary 'B' marks, U1 for its initial flights and was subsequently registered G-ACPC.

Variations on the Hawk design took many forms including the long-range single-seat machine, VT-AES (c/n 12). Built for an Indian owner, Mohan Singh, the M.2B was fitted with a 120 hp Hermes IV engine for an attempted record flight to Capetown, but it was written off in a forced landing in France during the initial stages of the flight in January 1934.

Miles built just one example of the M.2A Hawk which had a built-up rear fuselage and enclosed cabin structure. This was designed for S.B. Cliff to take part in the 1934 Egyptian Rally and was fitted with a 130 hp Gipsy III in-line engine and an enlarged rudder. Originally delivered in December 1933, it was destroyed in a fire at Brooklands three years later.

The Phillips & Powis organisation at Woodley grew rapidly and the garage background of the company was reflected in the 'service station' concept which helped to accelerate sales of the Hawk series. Here, an M.2H built to the order of Mrs B. MacDonald, sits outside the main sales and service hangar in early 1935.

The M.2F Hawk Major was a much improved Hawk with the more powerful 130 hp de Havilland Gipsy III engine and a new undercarriage with enclosed streamlined fairings. Hawk Majors took part in racing and long-distance competition and ZK-ADJ, ordered by the Manawatu Aero Club, set up a single-engined record to Australia in the 1934 MacRobertson Race, flown by Sqn Ldr M. MacGregor and H. Walker.

In 1934 Miles made the innovative move of equipping Hawk Majors with split trailing edge flaps which greatly improved the landing characteristics of the type. G-ACYX, built for J.A.H. Parker in December 1934, was the first M.2H and was subsequently exported to France as F-BCEX.

After the war, the airfield at Woodley continued to be a hive of activity not only for Miles Aircraft but also for the Reading Aero Club. M2F Hawk Major, G-ACYO, is seen in front of Sanford Manor on the edge of the aerodrome. Like many other civil aircraft, it was impressed into RAF service in 1943 and survived to return to civilian ownership when the war was over.

In this scene at Woodley, probably taken in 1933, Hawks are undergoing final assembly. These were the days before the concept of production lines and the aircraft were not only hand-built, but varied in detail from one machine to another.

The first M.2Y Hawk Trainer, G-ADZD, seen climbing out of Woodley in early 1936, was not impressed into the RAF at the outbreak of war. It remained as a civilian trainer with No. 8 ERFTS but only survived until the summer of 1940 when it was withdrawn from use.

Originally sold to H. Van Marken in 1935, the M.2H Hawk Major, G-ADMW was pressed into military service but withdrawn from use after an accident in 1943. Miles Aircraft rebuilt it after the war and it was later painted in a somewhat suspect wartime colour scheme with its original military serial number, DG590. This aircraft is now at Cardington in the hands of the RAF Museum – and hopefully will go on display before long.

Now preserved in the Chilean National Aeronautical Museum in Santiago, this M.2R Hawk Major is seen here shortly after delivery. The picture is thought to have been taken in 1937 – probably at an airstrip in the Andes – which no doubt explains the heavy flying suit worn by the pilot.

During 1934 and 1935 the production momentum built up at Woodley and additional hangar space was constructed to accommodate the main assembly section and to cope with the flow of aircraft being readied for customers. Here six new M.2W and M.2X Hawk Majors with shining engine cowlings and canvas covers over the cockpits and propellers await delivery to the Reserve Training School.

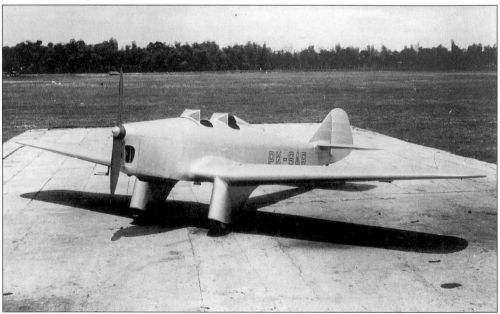

Miles exported almost half of its production of Hawk Majors and this M.2H, PK-SAR, was delivered to H.L. Krayenhoff in July 1935. It operated in the Dutch East Indies until it was impressed into service with the ML/KNIL on the outbreak of war. Its wartime service was short and it was withdrawn from operation and broken up in early 1942.

With the build-up to the war, Woodley saw the establishment of No. 8 Elementary Flying Training School and Miles produced the M.2W Hawk Trainer. This was a dual control Hawk Major and had a modified fin and overhung rudder. The first of four examples, G-ADWT, survived the war and is seen here at Luton, prior to being sold to Canada as CF-NXT in 1964.

The M.2X and M.2W were developed from the M.2H with larger cockpits to accommodate parachutes, a bigger wing and vacuum-operated flaps. The M.2X also had a larger and more rounded rudder with horn balancing. G-ADYZ was the first of nine production aircraft and it continued into the war years at Woodley until scrapped in August 1940.

The Phillips & Powis Reserve Training School at Woodley which was opened in November 1935, operated 13 Hawk Trainers and 8 Tiger Moths. This picture, taken in the immediate pre-war period, shows Hawk Trainers lined up in front of the modern purpose-built school. Unfortunately, the building had a short career and was destroyed by fire in October 1938.

In 1933, while production of the Hawk was starting to develop, Don Brown, George Miles and, it is believed, Geoffrey Wikner, designed a side-by-side two-seat pusher aircraft. It appears that the all-wood prototype was completed and fitted with a 95 hp Cirrus engine but never actually managed to achieve more than brief hops into the air.

# Two

# Racing and Touring

In the vibrant 1930s, the best advertisement for light aircraft was to be successful in the growing number of air racing events which took place. Miles Hawks soon appeared in the race line-ups and F.G. Miles was not slow in recognising the opportuntiy for publicity and recognition. Specially developed Hawks such as the Hawk Speed Six and the Sparrowhawk were built, marrying larger engines with the light wooden Hawk airframe to give sparkling performance. Phillips & Powis also built up its connections with the Royal Aircraft Establishment by supplying Sparrowhawks for use in aerodynamic research projects.

The next logical development was to build a larger aircraft with an enclosed cabin and so the Falcon was born. Once again, the three/four seat Falcon series and the later two-seat Whitney Straight captured customers, and racing honours. The prototype Falcon flew to Australia and the ebullient Tommy Rose took a Falcon Six to Capetown and back. The Miles imagination conceived the Merlin air taxi aircraft and also the twin-engined Peregrine in a period of rapid expansion for the Woodley-based firm. One of the most famous aircraft of this pre-war era was the Miles Mohawk which was built to the order of Charles Lindbergh, who was known the world over for his 1927 pioneering crossing of the Atlantic from New York to Paris in the Ryan NYP.

Specially built for Sir Charles Rose, to race in the 1934 King's Cup, the M.2E Gipsy Six Hawk, G-ACTE, was a development of the Hawk Major fitted with a de Havilland Gipsy Six engine and a single-seat cockpit. Subsequently retitled Hawk Speed Six, it had to retire with engine trouble in the 1934 race but went on to complete the 1935 King's Cup contest. In January 1937 it is believed to have been delivered to the Republican side in the Spanish Civil War.

The prototype M.2F Hawk Major, G-ACTD, which first flew in 1934, was the first model to use the Gipsy III engine in the Hawk airframe. Miles subsequently removed the front cockpit to create a single-seat racer which was entered in the 1934 King's Cup Air Race and finished second with an overall speed of 147.78 mph, piloted by Tommy Rose. G-ACTD was destroyed in a crash at Doncaster two years later.

Two examples of the M.2T were built by Miles Aircraft for the fourteenth annual King's Cup race of 1935, which was flown over a 1,300 mile course starting at Hatfield and touching Edinburgh and Belfast. This variant had a Hawk Major airframe with a single open cockpit and a 150 hp Cirrus Major R engine. G-ADNJ, flown by Alex Henshaw, experienced engine trouble over the Irish Sea and is seen here with a rescue boat in attendance off Malin Head.

Only one M.2S Hawk Major was built. Registered G-ADLH, it was equipped with long-range tanks and a single-seat cockpit with a small bubble canopy. In 1937, the aircraft was purchased by Govind P. Nair, an Indian gentleman who planned to fly to Brazil via Dakar and then home via New York. Mr Nair left Croydon on 28 October 1937, but the trip ended suddenly when the Hawk Major crashed on landing at Forges-les-Eaux in France, killing the pilot.

The strength of the Miles challenge in air races of the 1930s is well illustrated by this line-up of 13 aircraft at Reading prior to the 1935 King's Cup. In the foreground are Sparrowhawk G-ADNL, Hawk Speed Six G-ADOD, Hawk Majors G-ADLB, G-ADLN, G-ADNK, the Gipsy-Six Hawk G-ACTE and Falcon Six G-ADLC, which won the race, piloted by Flt Lt Tommy Rose at an average speed of 176 mph.

The M.2L Hawk Speed Six, G-ADGP, was the only one of the three aircraft built to survive the war. Ordered by Luis Fontes it had a similar airframe to that of the first aircraft, G-ADOD, but had a 200 hp Gipsy Six 1F engine. After the war it was fitted with an enlarged cockpit canopy and, in the hands of Ron Paine, won the SBAC Challenge Cup in 1958, 1959 and 1964, and the 1959 Air League Challenge Cup.

Hawk Speed Six, G-ADGP, passed through several hands after its ownership by Ron Paine. It now resides in the Shuttleworth Collection at Old Warden, where it has been restored by Ron Souch with a copy of the original pre-war cockpit canopy.

The M.5 Sparrowhawk was a special long-range racing Hawk variant built for F.G. Miles to compete in the 1935 King's Cup race. It was a single-seater with a fuselage of reduced depth and length with short-span wings and a wide-track undercarriage. It was fitted with a 140 hp de Havilland Gipsy Major engine and performed well, although it was handicapped and lost out in the arduous Round Britain Race. G-ADNL was later converted into the Sparrowjet.

The two Hawk Majors, G-ADLB and G-ADLN, flown respectively by Lt O. Cathcart-Jones and Flg Officer R.A. Edwards, take off at Hatfield in the King's Cup race on 6 September 1935, *en route* for the first reporting point at Newcastle. In a major *coup* for Miles, G-ADLN finished in second place, with G-ADLB taking third place and the race being won by Tommy Rose in a Falcon Six.

The third of five production Sparrowhawks, G-AELT, flew in the summer of 1936. Painted in dark blue, it took part in the 1936 Schlesinger Air Race from Portsmouth to Johannesburg but fell out of the race due to engine trouble at Khartoum. It eventually arrived in South Africa where it was registered ZS-ANO and fitted with a raised rear fuselage and enclosed cockpit canopy.

In the early part of the war, the Royal Aircraft Establishment took delivery of two M.5 Sparrowhawks for use in the development of high lift double-slotted flaps, including this example which carried the Phillips & Powis 'B' mark U3 and is seen here in military camouflage. After the war this aircraft was civilianised as G-AGDL and was subsequently destroyed at Tollerton in 1948.

The second of the pair of RAE Sparrowhawks carried the identity U5 and in this photograph, taken at an early stage of its career, the undercarriage fairings have not been fitted. Also evident is the system of large twin flaps taking up almost the full wing span. This Sparrowhawk was broken up at Woodley in 1942.

This photograph of the M.7 Nighthawk U5 provides an interesting comparison with the Sparrowhawk U5 and shows how Phillips & Powis reused the temporary registration markings on several aircraft. The style of 'U' marks was changed at the beginning of the war to a four-digit number and these were not reused in the same way.

With the success of the Hawk, F.G. Miles saw the need for an aircraft with a completely enclosed cabin and designed the four-seat M.3 Falcon Major. In this view of the main assembly hangar at Woodley a production M.3A, carrying 'B' marks, is being rolled out and other Falcons and Hawk Majors are in various stages of completion in the background.

The prototype M.3 Falcon, G-ACTM, was a two-seater with a streamlined windscreen. Built for Mr H.L. Brook, it was fitted with a Gipsy Major engine salvaged from his Puss Moth G-ABXY, which had crashed in the Alps. Brook flew the Falcon to Australia in the October 1934 MacRobertson Race - and then flew it back in March 1935, in a record 7 days, 19 hours. The aircraft was written off in an accident 18 months later.

The production M.3A Falcon Major differed from the prototype in having a wider fuselage to give a full four-seat cabin. It had a solid rear cabin roof, the patent forward-sloped windscreen designed by Miles to give improved vision and streamlining, and a modified engine cowling to enclose its 130 hp Gipsy Major. G-ADHG was built in 1935 and sold to Australia, where it became VH-AAT.

The Falcon VH-AAT remained active in Australia for many years in the hands of Les Hatfield, at Casey Airfield, not far from Melbourne. In this photograph, taken at the 1991 Air Show to celebrate the 70th Anniversary of the RAAF, the upward folding cabin door is well illustrated. At that time, it had been painted as G-ACTM for a TV programme to represent the Falcon prototype but it has now reverted to VH-AAT.

Miles sold one of the 19 production Falcon Majors to Nordisk Aerotjanst in Sweden, where it flew as SE-AFN for many years. Between 1940 and 1944 it also served with the Swedish Air Force. It was restored to the British register and is seen here at Sywell in May 1966, adorned in a silver and yellow colour scheme.

The M.3A Falcon Major, G-AEEG, just after work had been completed on its restoration to the British register in 1962. Clearly visible is the structure of the undercarriage legs prior to the installation of the enclosed speed fairings. G-AEEG still flies in the UK and is owned by Skysport Engineering.

The fifteenth production M.3A Falcon Major, G-AENG, seen here flying near Woodley, had an unusual and short-lived career. Completed in September 1936, it was entered in the 1937 King's Cup Air Race. Flown by Wg Cdr Sherren and Wg Cdr Hilton, the Falcon ran into a severe down-draught while turning at Scarborough Castle and the two crew were thrown through the cabin roof as the aircraft headed for the ground.

The Miles M.3B Falcon Six was a development of the Falcon Major with a 200 hp de Havilland Gipsy Six engine, the first of which, G-ADLC, was completed in July 1935. It competed in the 1935 King's Cup and took its pilot, Tommy Rose, to victory with an average speed of 176.28 mph over the 1,300 mile course.

In February 1936, Flt Lt Tommy Rose, seen here in front of the prototype Falcon Six, set off from Lympne and established a new record of 3 days, 17 hours for the 7,300 mile flight to Cape Town. Rose then flew G-ADLC back to England, also breaking the Cape Town – London record. He later joined Miles as sales manager and then chief test pilot.

Seventeen examples of the Falcon Six were built, one of the final production aircraft being G-AEAO, built in 1936. This M.3B was quickly sold to Holland but returned to serve with the RAF during the war. After post-war civil operation in England as G-AGZX, it went to Belgium and then to France, as F-BBCN. It is seen here at Lognes-Emerainville in September 1967, fitted with a non-standard cabin roof and windscreen.

The Royal Aircraft Establishment acquired M.3B Falcon Six, K5924 as a test aircraft for Piercy laminar flow wing experiments. The Reading factory constructed four sets of wings with different thickness/chord ratios. This aircraft is seen here at the time of initial delivery fitted with standard M.3B wings

The RAE's Falcon Six subsequently received a camouflage paint scheme and this illustration shows it fitted with one of the alternative wings with shorter root fillets provided for the experiments. It was also modified with a smaller fin and an overhung rudder. K5924 was eventually struck off charge in April 1944.

The last Falcon Six was delivered to the Royal Aircraft Establishment in 1938 to be used in experiments on highly tapered wings and carried the serial number L9705. After the war it was further modified, as shown here, with a taller undercarriage attached to the fuselage, which was necessary to raise the angle of attack when taking off with the special wing it was testing.

Falcon L9705 was nicknamed the 'Gillette Falcon' as a result of the sharp leading edge of its experimental wing. This biconvex wing was built of wood to simulate the wing which was to be used on the supersonic Miles M.52. It was extremely thin in section and, even though flaps were fitted, the landing speed of the Falcon was extremely high.

Phillips & Powis built just four examples of the M.4 Merlin. It was a five-seat aircraft – essentially a scaled up Falcon Six - and was powered by the same 200 hp Gipsy Six engine despite its higher gross weight. The first Merlin, G-ADFE, seen here, was built to the order of Birkett Air Services who used it as an air taxi, and two were also sold to Tata Airways in India.

In 1936, Miles designed an eight-seat twin-engined machine, the M.8 Peregrine. Again, it was powered by Gipsy Six engines and had a retractable undercarriage. Only two Peregrines were built, the prototype, U9, seen here, and an experimental boundary layer wing research aircraft for the RAE. No further production was undertaken due to increasing pressure on the factory capacity at Woodley.

The M.6 Hawcon was a one-off prototype built by Phillips & Powis for the Royal Aircraft Establishment for research into the aerodynamics of wings with very deep aerofoil sections. It was mostly a modified Falcon Six airframe with some other Hawk components (resulting in the Hawcon name) and had two seats and a cockpit with a streamlined windscreen and larger side windows.

The Hawcon K5925 is seen here fitted with one of its three sets of interchangeable long span wings and the deep wing root profile is evident. It had quite a brief career with the RAE from 1936 until May 1939, when it undershot on landing at Farnborough during flap trials and was written off.

The Miles M.7 Nighthawk was a development of the Falcon Six, intended for RAF instrument flying training, with dual controls for the front two seats and a single rear seat. One Nighthawk, L6846, was built for the RAF and this formed the basis for the production M.16 Mentor. This aircraft has the earlier rear window shape of the production Falcon Six.

Miles built a total of five M.7A Nighthawks including a pair of aircraft delivered to the Rumanian Air Force. One aircraft, seen here in 1940 in the Class 'B' markings, U5 and an early war camouflage scheme, was fitted with wings designed for the M.12 Mohawk. The smaller rear window is evident and this aircraft was fitted with a variable pitch propeller.

The Nighthawk with Mohawk wings was a four-seater and was fitted with a 205 hp Gipsy Six Srs. II engine. In this picture, the variable pitch propeller has been fitted with a streamlined spinner. Miles retained the aircraft as a company transport and it is seen here in its post-war livery, registered G-AGWT.

The Miles company 'hack' Nighthawk was eventually sold to an owner in Kenya and later flew as VR-TCM with Steel Bros. Ltd in Tanganyika. In this photograph, taken at Denham in 1962, the Nighthawk was on its way back to a new British owner. In the following year it left for Singapore but had technical problems and was abandoned at Marseilles.

Tests with the Nighthawk led to the RAF placing an order for 45 examples of a modified version designated M.16 Mentor with modified cabin windows, a deeper fuselage and an enlarged tailplane with large anti-spin strakes. The second prototype, seen here, was eventually written off in 1944 due to a damaged mainspar resulting from a heavy landing at Boscombe Down.

The Mentor went into service with the RAF, primarily in the communications role. The camouflaged aircraft in this photograph, L4428, started service life with No.1 Electrical and Wireless School and later served with the Usworth Station Flight. Initial production aircraft were fitted with a Nighthawk rudder but L4428 has the larger rudder which was fitted retrospectively to the Mentor fleet.

In 1936, demand for a modern two-seat aircraft to meet the needs of flying clubs resulted in F.G. Miles designing the M.11 Straight Special. This was named after Whitney Straight, who planned a chain of aero clubs and required an enclosed cabin in the aircraft they would use. G-AERV, seen here over Berkshire, was an early example of the production Whitney Straight.

One of the early Whitney Straights, G-AEUJ, was acquired by Hawker Aircraft Ltd early in the war and was used as a company communications aircraft until 1957. Seen here in a muddy corner of Baginton Airport in the winter of 1966, G-AEUJ was withdrawn from use in 1970 and is currently under restoration in the hands of Bob Mitchell.

The prototype Whitney Straight, G-AECT, was used to carry out further experiments on boundary layer control following the work done with the BLS Peregrine. This involved fitting a section of aerofoil round the wing of the aircraft, together with large wing fences and an under-wing venturi to provide suction at the wing surface.

A total of 50 Whitney Straights left the Miles factory during 1936, 1937 and 1938. G-AFGK spent the war as a communications aircraft for Airwork and resided at Elstree for many subsequent years. It was eventually sold to an American buyer in 1977.

The successor to the Whitney Straight was the Miles M.17 Monarch which went into production in 1938. The prototype, G-AFCR, is seen here in a publicity photo in front of the Falcon Hotel at Woodley, with an appropriate model sitting in the open entry door. In the background is the Miles' Rolls Royce Phantom II with its Barker saloon coachwork.

Only 11 Monarchs were built before wartime Magister production took priority over civil aircraft orders. G-AFLW was completed in November 1938, and spent many years as the Rolls Royce communications aircraft. Sold to Rex Coates and painted with SAS airline colours, it is seen here in 1977 at White Waltham, where it is currently stored.

One of the last production Monarchs, G-AFRZ, owned by Lord Douglas-Hamilton, was impressed into RAF service and flew with Vickers Armstrongs. After the war it became G-AIDE and is seen here at Stapleford Tawney. The Monarch used Magister wings and G-AIDE also acquired additional rear windows, which were not standard on the type.

The similarity between the Monarch and the Whitney Straight is evident in this picture of French registered Whitney Straight, F-APPZ, taken at Shoreham in the 1950s. This aircraft was formerly G-AEWT but was sold to France in 1937.

49

Miles was asked by Col Charles Lindbergh, seen here talking to George Miles, to build a fast two-seat aircraft in which he could travel around Europe in order to locate landing fields for Pan American Airways' route network. Miles designed the M.12 Mohawk, powered by a 200 hp Menasco Buccaneer in-line engine, which was painted in a distinctive black and orange colour scheme and made its maiden flight at Woodley on 22 August 1936.

The Mohawk took Lindbergh, seen here in the front seat, on trips as far afield as India and Russia. It was impressed during the war but was of limited value to the RAF due to the overheating of the Menasco engine. After the war it was converted with open cockpits. It crashed in Spain in January 1950 and the remains were acquired by L.S. Casey and taken to the United States for restoration and static exhibition.

The success of Miles aircraft in the air races of the mid 1930s resulted in a tiny single-seat racer being built for the 1937 King's Cup. The M.13 Hobby, registered U2, was driven by a 140 hp Gipsy Major engine with a variable pitch propeller; it was the first Miles racer to have a retractable undercarriage.

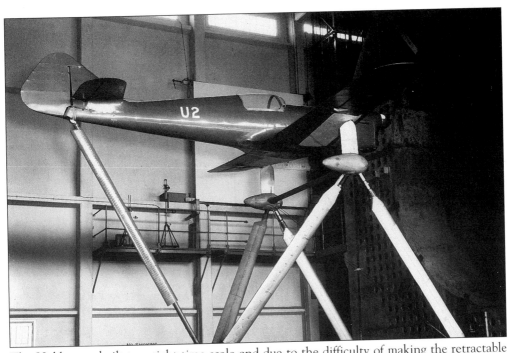

The Hobby was built to a tight time scale and due to the difficulty of making the retractable undercarriage function properly, it failed to take part in the King's Cup race. The Hobby was eventually sold to the RAE as an aerodynamic test vehicle and was small enough to be used in the wind tunnel at Farnborough, as shown here.

Expansion of the Woodley Aerodrome manufacturing complex during the late 1930s included the construction of new offices for Phillips & Powis Aircraft Ltd. Designed by Guy Morgan and Partners, these were very modern for their day and continue to be used by Adwest Group plc. The lights shown in this 1939 night-time picture were soon to be extinguished as the blackout conditions of war arrived.

# Three
# Training for War

*As war became inevitable, Miles emerged as a leading provider of training aircraft for the RAF during a phase of frenetic expansion for the military establishment. Initial production was concentrated on the M.14 Magister basic trainer, but the foresight of F.G. Miles resulted in the private venture Kestrel which became the Master I advanced trainer. The company received large orders for this aircraft. Great changes took place in the manufacturing techniques adopted by Phillips & Powis with new systems of construction jigging and a moving assembly line system coming into use.*

*As the war progressed, Miles flew a number of new prototypes and added additional production models. The M.20 fighter was particularly well conceived – even though it did not progress beyond the prototype stage. The concept of sub-assembly allowed many parts of the aircraft to be built in factories remote from the Woodley site. This necessitated the creation of increased manufacturing space and several new factories were opened, including a large facility at South Marston near Swindon and an assembly centre at Doncaster to cope with Master production. Employment expanded rapidly and the open management practices of Miles resulted in a co-operative atmosphere which contributed greatly to the wartime total output of 6,367 aircraft, most of which required a high level of craft skill resulting from their all-wood design.*

A line-up of Master I trainers awaits delivery to the RAF from the Miles factory at Woodley.

With war clouds gathering, F.G. Miles saw the need for an advanced training aircraft to be used in teaching new pilots for the Hurricanes and Spitfires which were in production. The M.9 PV Trainer was built with Phillips & Powis's own resources using a Kestrel XVI engine provided by Rolls Royce. The prototype is seen here painted up for the RAF display at Hendon, held in the summer of 1937.

The M.9 prototype, later named Kestrel, made its first flight on 3 June 1937. It underwent various changes to its tail unit and to the cockpit canopy design. In this photograph the rear windows have been removed and a new centre canopy structure installed. The registration U5 has again been used (see page 33).

The Kestrel prototype had tandem seating with the pupil in the front cockpit and the instructor behind. Unfortunately, on the landing approach the instructor was unable to see much more than the pupil's head! The solution was a rear seat which could be raised and a hinged windshield, seen here being demonstrated by F.G. Miles as the student and chief test pilot, Bill Skinner, in the back.

The Kestrel after modifications to the radiator and the fitting of the Master I production standard cockpit and the taller vertical tail unit. At this stage, the aircraft was still painted in silver, but had received service markings N3300 and was later painted in a camouflage colour scheme.

The Kestrel was developed into the M.9 Master I with further alterations being made to the cockpit canopy and the engine air intake. During the later stages of its test programme the Kestrel was fitted with the leading edge slats seen here. This modification was not incorporated on production Master Is.

The first production Master I is seen during its initial engine runs at Woodley. At this juncture the engine air intake was positioned under the nose but the initial test flight showed the aircraft to be nose-heavy. As a consequence, the radiator was repositioned under the wing centre section and this solved the centre of gravity problem.

The first production Master I, in RAF camouflage and with the repositioned radiator, flies over Berkshire during its flight test phase. It was first flown on 31 March 1939 by F.G. Miles and was followed by 897 further production examples.

Master I, N7427, seen here prior to delivery, was delivered in November 1939 but only achieved one year of service with No. 5 Service Flying Training School. It experienced an engine failure during a training sortie in November 1940 and hit trees during its emergency landing at Coddington Malpas, Cheshire.

Initial examples of the Master I had a hinged front cockpit canopy, but this was replaced with a sliding canopy from the 204th aircraft as a result of the vulnerability to damage experienced by the original design. This gave rise to a slightly altered roof line and a new windshield with a more sloping front section, as shown on this view of N7947 in use by 9 FTS at Hullavington.

Master I, N7683, awaits delivery to its RAF user, No. 5 SFTS. In the background is the camouflaged Miles factory at Woodley with a sandbagged gun emplacement on the right and the tail of the prototype Miles M.18 Mk.1 just visible on the left. This was one of the last Masters with the hinged cockpit canopy.

With the Battle of Britain looming, Miles produced 24 single-seat M.24 Master Fighters equipped with six 0.303 mm Browning guns. The modified rear cockpit transparencies are shown in this picture of N7809 taken prior to delivery. It went to 5 SFTS in June 1940 and ended its life as an instructional airframe at No. 5 School of Technical Training.

Master IA, N7685, is seen here at Woodley prior to delivery to the RAF. It was the first aircraft with the sliding canopy and served with No. 5 Flying Training School, then with No. 7 PAFU, before being withdrawn from service in March 1944.

In this photograph, taken in the summer of 1939 at Woodley, Miles on the right is seen conversing earnestly with Blossom. The aircraft is believed to be the third prototype Master I, N7410, and sitting on the wing is chief test pilot, Bill Skinner, who tragically died in his bath in the following November following a brain haemorrhage. The tail of this aircraft appears to be tied down with a stout piece of rope and the yellow outer ring of the early roundel is clearly seen merging with the trainer yellow underside of the aircraft.

The Master I was succeeded by the M.19 Master II. The airframe stayed essentially the same but the Master II was fitted with an 870 hp Bristol Mercury XX radial engine which substantially altered its appearance. This Master II, AZ168, was sent to South Africa for the Joint Air Training Scheme, but weather conditions resulted in warping of the wooden airframes and Masters were not a success in South African service.

In mid 1940, due to an anticipated shortage of Bristol Mercury engines, Miles fitted the Master with an 825 hp Pratt & Whitney Wasp Junior engine. With this engine installed it became the M.27 Master III, and the shorter engine cowling of this version is clear in this view of W8513. All Master IIIs were built at the South Marston factory.

Master III, DL630, was one of the early production aircraft, and is seen here during its pre-delivery test flight. This Master was used initially by 286 Squadron which provided a variety of aircraft for target towing and target training for army gunners. It was eventually withdrawn from use and scrapped in November 1945.

After the war a number of Masters continued to operate in the RAF. This Master II, W9056, spent the whole of its service life with the Central Gunnery School and is seen here wearing its post-war identity code letters and markings. It was finally retired in June 1950. A total of 1,747 Master IIs were built, including 488 produced at South Marston. Some were used as glider tugs.

The Air Ministry issued a new specification in 1936 for a two-seat elementary trainer. The Miles M.2Y Hawk Trainer was already in service with No. 8 ERFTS and Miles devised a modified version with full blind flying instrumentation and larger cockpits to allow the instructor and pupil to wear parachutes. L5945, seen here at Woodley, was one of the first batch of M.14s to be delivered.

The M.14 was initially known as the Hawk Trainer but soon received the RAF name Magister. In this picture of a line of early Magisters the narrow undercarriage fairings which distinguished the M.14 from the M.2Y are clearly shown. Once the Magister entered service these fairings were often removed to improve maintenance access.

The fifth production Magister, L5916, was delivered to the Central Flying School in 1937 and was painted in a distinctive colour scheme as part of a proposed formation display team. It served with a number of units including 1 FTS, 61 Squadron and 245 Squadron. Some of its time was spent at Exeter with 308 Squadron and as the Exeter Station 'hack'; it ended its life as an instructional airframe.

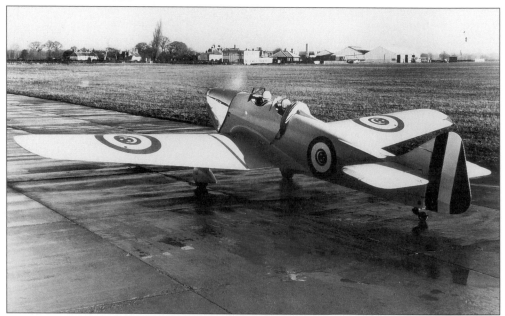

A batch of 33 Magisters was delivered to Egypt, some of these being diverted from RAF production allocations. In this fine picture of one of the first Egyptian machines the folding blind flying hood on the rear cockpit is evident. This aircraft has the early rudder shape which was inherited from the original Hawk Trainer.

Another recipient of Magisters was the Irish Air Force which received eighteen ex-RAF aircraft which were refurbished by Miles Aircraft during 1945 and 1946. Three of the Irish aircraft were destroyed in service and the last Magister was retired from flying operations at Baldonnel in 1952, when the IAC acquired Percival Provost trainers as replacements.

One of the remaining airworthy Magisters is P6382, which is maintained by the Shuttleworth Trust in flying condition. It has been rebuilt at Old Warden using major components of two Hawk Trainer IIIs – G-AJRS and G-AJDR. From 1938, Magisters were fitted with a taller rudder, as seen here, in order to improve the type's spinning characteristics.

Another surviving Magister is V1075, whose restoration has been completed by Adrian Brook at Shoreham. Restored in an early wartime all-yellow colour scheme, this Magister, which has a fully spatted undercarriage, has been assembled with parts from three Magisters – G-AKPF, G-AHYL and N3788.

Miles used a standard production Magister, P6456, to experiment with a crosswind landing gear system. Known as the Maclaren Undercarriage this provided a swivelling mechanism for the main gear legs so they could be set at an angle. The aircraft could then be flown into wind on final approach but touch down along the runway direction. In practice the system was not successful and development was abandoned.

After the war, many Magisters were declared surplus and 234 were refurbished by Miles under the name M.14A Hawk Trainer III. This Hawk Trainer was operated for many years by the Scottish Flying Club and then moved to the Denham Flying Club, until being retired and then incorporated into the rebuild of the Shuttleworth Magister.

A familiar sight at Biggin Hill in the late-1950s was this pale blue Hawk Trainer III, G-AKAS, operated by the Experimental Flying Group together with sister ship, G-AITN. It lacks the undercarriage fairings and spats and the blind flying hood of the military Magister. G-AKAS was finally withdrawn from use in June 1961.

Even the Magister was eligible as a racing aircraft and G-AIUA was one of several machines to be modified as a single-seater with the rear cockpit faired over. This aircraft was a regular mount for C.A. Nepean Bishop in the King's Cup and other races of the early 1950s.

One of many hard working Hawk Trainer IIIs with post-war private owners was G-AHUJ, seen here in the hangar of its long term home at Scone in July 1962. It was subsequently taken over by the Strathallan Aircraft Collection and is currently airworthy.

Always the supporting act for F.G. Miles, George Miles served the company as chief engineer and is seen here in front of an early production Magister. The gleaming cowling is notable and the folding blind flying hood can be seen behind the rear cockpit.

In February 1939, Miles flew the first of two prototypes of the M.15 Trainer in response to the Air Ministry specification T.1/37. The first aircraft, seen here, was powered by a 200 hp Gipsy Six engine but the performance of the aircraft was poor due to the unrealistic official specification and the M.15 did not go into production.

With the Magister in widespread service with the RAF, Walter Capley designed an improved trainer known as the M.18. It was powered by the same Gipsy Major engine as the Magister but had a new wing with constant chord, which improved its handling characteristics. The prototype, marked U2, made its maiden flight in the hands of Miles on 4 December 1938.

During testing, the vertical fin of the M.18 prototype was moved forwards. The aircraft was also fitted with a tricycle undercarriage. This involved the elimination of the front cockpit to house the nosewheel leg fitting, but Miles retained the tailwheel as a safety measure.

The second of the four M.18s was registered U8 and it was fitted with a larger rudder, a spatted undercarriage and a 150 hp Cirrus Minor III engine, which gave it improved maximum speed performance. This M.18 was used extensively by Miles Aircraft during the war years as a communications machine.

After the war, the second M.18 was sold by Miles Aircraft. Registered G-AHKY, it was painted in a cream colour scheme and flown to victory by Brian Iles in three major air races, including the 1961 King's Cup.

Another variation on the M.18 theme was the third aircraft, U-0238 which, while being structurally identical to the second machine, was fitted with an enclosed cockpit canopy. It too was sold to a private owner after the war, as G-AHOA, but was written off in a crash at Littondale in Yorkshire in May 1950.

The last M.18 was built by Miles as an aerodynamic test vehicle for a range of low-speed control devices to be used on a proposed Supermarine naval aircraft and was delivered to the Royal Aircraft Establishment at Farnborough. The M.18HL had large leading edge slats and complex flaps incorporating the ailerons. Here the guide mechanism for the large full span slotted flaps is well shown.

In this later picture of the M.18HL, it has been fitted with upturned wingtips to improve stability during testing. It has also been fitted with a large triangular tail unit. Tests with these many additional features revealed that the proposed naval design would not meet the stable slow speed characteristics being sought by the RAE.

The arrival of the Second World War put pressure on the production of the sophisticated and expensive Spitfires and Hurricanes. F.G. Miles saw an opportunity to design a single-seat fighter which would be cheaper to produce and could be built in much larger quantities. His solution was the Miles M.20. The first of two prototypes, marked U9, is seen here.

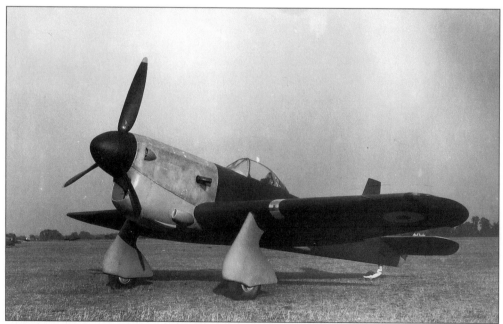

The prototype M.20 was built and flown in the amazing time of 65 days. Simple as it was, with a fixed undercarriage and many parts from the Miles Master, the M.20 was able to match the performance of the Hawker Hurricane. Here it is seen prior to receiving its camouflage paint and its rudder.

The first flight of the prototype M.20 was on 15 September 1940. Tommy Rose, appointed as chief test pilot after the death of Bill Skinner, flew the M.20, painted in its test registration U9, from Woodley, and it was immediately clear that it could be a potent addition to the RAF's front line fighter force.

A second prototype of the all-wood M.20 was built to a naval specification as U-0228. This still used the 1,300 hp Rolls Royce Merlin XX engine, but differed externally from the first aircraft in having modified undercarriage fairings and a sharper propeller spinner.

Sadly, the Battle of Britain was over before the M.20 could be called into action and no production order was placed for the Miles fighter. The M.20 prototype, now carrying the RAF serial number AX834 and flown by Hugh Kennedy, ended its days in the gravel pit at the end of the Woodley main runway after skidding on icy ground in the winter of 1940.

With many Master IIs and IIIs in service, the versatile airframe was developed into the M.25 Martinet. Using a Master II airframe, Miles moved the engine forwards and installed a target towing winch and longer cockpit canopy to create a useful target tug. The prototype, LR241, is seen here at Woodley early in its trials period.

The Martinet HP165 started its RAF career in August 1942 with No. 7 OTU. It is seen here at Shorts Northern Ireland factory where it was repaired following an accident. HP165 subsequently went into storage and was scrapped in 1948, without further operational service.

This picture of Martinet HN862 illustrates the black and yellow under-wing markings applied to target towing aircraft. A total of 1,724 Martinets was completed by Miles. In addition, 65 Queen Martinet pilotless targets were also produced.

At the end of the war, Miles put forward a proposal to the Air Ministry for the Miles Martinet target tug to be converted as a trainer. The rear cockpit would be raised and fitted with a bubble canopy to provide good forward vision for the instructor. A plywood mock-up of the proposed modification was fitted to Martinet HP413, as seen here.

The M.37 Advanced Trainer had good flying qualities and would have been a very satisfactory aircraft for the RAF. Two prototypes were built, the first of which, JN275 is seen here, but the Air Ministry was also moving forward with the new Percival Prentice and the Boulton Paul Balliol trainer, both with side-by-side seating, and the Miles proposal was not adopted for production.

The M.33 Monitor was the largest wartime aircraft built by Miles Aircraft and was designed as a high speed target tug, primarily for use by the Royal Navy. It was the first Miles aircraft to use metal construction – for the fuselage, although the wings were made of wood. The prototype, NF900, seen here, first flew on 5 April 1944.

Some idea of the expansion at Woodley during the war years is clear from this photograph of Miles Monitors on the production line in late 1944. The metal fuselage and wooden wings have been joined at this stage and installation of the engines is under way.

The second production Monitor, NP407, clearly shows the slim rear fuselage and two 1,700 hp Wright Cyclone engines. The under-fuselage hatch incorporated a moving belt system for releasing the target. Not shown in this picture is the transparent dome on the upper fuselage to allow the winch operator to control the target equipment.

With the end of the war, Monitor production was severely cut back and eventually, only 20 of the intended 600 M.33 aircraft were completed in addition to the two prototypes. This picture of seven Monitors is believed to have been taken at Market Harborough, where Miles apparently stored production Martinets and Monitors prior to delivery.

One of the many engineering innovations produced by Miles during the war was the electronic actuator. It was used to power the trim tabs on the Monitor and the undercarriage on the Gemini. A separate actuator division was created by Miles Aircraft to manufacture the actuator for many industrial purposes, and it became the most successful product of the Adwest Group after the war.

The early part of the war produced demands for a wide variety of aircraft including communications types. Miles was very experienced in small two- and four-seat tourers and George Miles and Ray Bournon developed the M.28 at Liverpool Road. The prototype, U-0232, was also designated LR.1 and is seen here showing its unusual 'kneeling' undercarriage configuration.

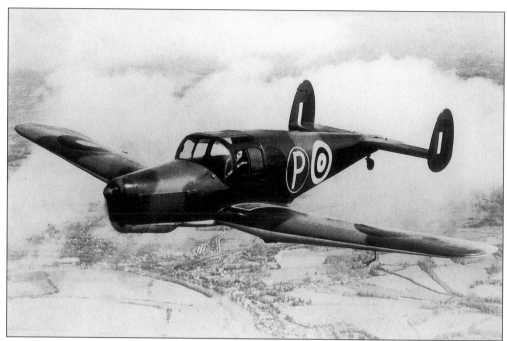

The M.28 prototype first flew on 11 July 1941. It is seen here over Reading, being flown by George Miles. It was the first Miles single-engined light aircraft to have a retractable undercarriage and was powered by a 130 hp Gipsy Major I engine. Miles intended that dual control would be fitted to allow the M.28 to be used as a trainer.

The second M.28 Mk.II, here wearing its military serial, HM583, had a more powerful 140 hp Gipsy Major IIA engine and additional rear 'lozenge' shaped windows. After the war it was sold in Australia.

The M.28 Mk. III was built with three sets of controls, including a student's position in one of the rear seats, equipped with a stick and rudder pedals. This aircraft, U-0242, also had a new undercarriage with straight oleo legs and large square rear windows.

Miles built a Mk.IV version of the M.28 which first flew in 1944 and had a further power increase, using the 145 hp Gipsy Major IIA driving a constant speed propeller. Painted in an overall blue colour scheme, it was used by Miles Aircraft for communications for the remainder of the war.

The last of six Miles M.28 Mercury monoplanes was completed in 1946 as a civil aircraft and was registered G-AHAA. This variant had a thinner section wing which had been introduced on the third M.28, and resulted in the main wheels protruding when the undercarriage was retracted. This M.28 remains airworthy with an owner in Denmark.

The M.28 Mk. IV was refurbished by Miles in 1947 and sold to Switzerland. It is seen here at Woodley with its Swiss tail colours and registration, HB-EED, just before delivery. It passed subsequently to new owners in Australia.

Although the M.28 was a promising light aircraft with good performance, it was the M.38 Messenger which reached series production, initially as an army air observation post machine. The first M.28/38 Messenger, U-0223, was converted from the M.28 prototype. It had a fixed undercarriage and external flaps and was flown initially with a twin fin/rudder assembly.

Several different tail unit configurations were tested on U-0223, the Messenger M.38/28 prototype, following its first flight on 12 September 1942. These included the wire-braced single fin and rudder shown here. Eventually, Miles settled on a triple fin arrangement for the production M.38.

Messengers delivered to the RAF had square rear windows, as seen on the first pre-production aircraft, RG327. This Messenger made its maiden flight on 3 July 1944 and was painted in a photographic reconnaissance blue colour scheme. Following testing at Boscombe Down it flew with the Metropolitan Communication Squadron until being civilianised in 1948.

One of the roles envisaged for the Messenger by George Miles was as a light defence aircraft to be carried on the back of merchant ships. The M.28/38 prototype, renamed Mariner for the purpose, was used for tests with a deck arrester cable system.

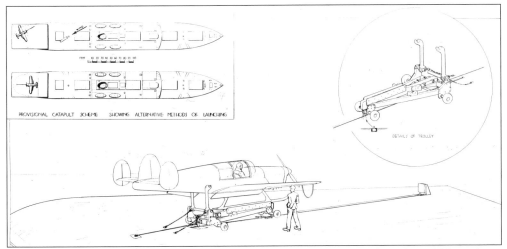

A more radical version of the Mariner was to be equipped with skids and would have been catapulted off the rear deck of a cargo vessel in order to carry out anti-submarine patrols. This Miles drawing shows the M.38 on its launching dolly.

Recovery of the M.38 following an anti-submarine sortie involved flying the aircraft into a net with a hole in the middle, which could be quickly erected on the deck of the parent ship. The Messenger prototype was used for tests of this system and flew into the large net set up on the Woodley runway. The system was not adopted by the Royal Navy.

The Messengers delivered to the RAF ended up being used for communications rather than as AOPs. The most famous user was Field Marshall Montgomery, who used three Messengers including RG333, which crashed following engine failure with 'Monty' on board. The third Messenger, RH378, shown here, has the Field Marshall's five stars painted on the tail.

'Monty' is seen here sitting in the cockpit of one of the Messengers during operations in France, probably in late 1944.

Miles flew one modified Messenger, which was designated M.48. This machine, U-0247, seen here over Woodley in a PR blue colour scheme, had a 150 hp Cirrus Major engine and electrically operated retractable flaps in place of the standard external flaps of the normal Messenger. These modifications were found to add little to the M.48's performance.

This view taken at Woodley in 1944 shows the M.28 Mk. IV, U-0243, at the head of a lineup containing the Miles M.48 and three production RAF Miles M.38 Messengers.

Typical of the post-war Messengers built at Newtownards was G-AILI. Completed in late 1946, it was used for some while as the personal aircraft of George Miles and was tested with a Praga E engine. It then passed through the hands of several owners before being written off in a landing accident at Beauvais in May 1964.

Messenger 2A, G-AKBO, has the distinction of being the winner of the 1954 King's Cup Air Race. Flown by Flt Lt Harold Wood, it completed the circuit at Baginton at a speed of 133 mph. This Messenger is still flying with Clive du Cros – 50 years after it left the Miles factory in Northern Ireland.

The square windows on Australian Messenger VH-WYN identify it as a former RAF aircraft. VH-WYN is now complete after a long period of restoration and is an exhibit at the Wangaratta Air Museum situated to the north of Melbourne in Australia.

A rare visitor to White Waltham in 1962 for overhaul was the Spanish-registered Messenger, EC-ACU. It was originally delivered to Spain in August 1947, and is now believed to be in storage awaiting a rebuild.

The early RAF Messengers were all built at Reading and the production line was set up at the Northern Ireland factory once civil production commenced. G-ALAH is the ninth production military aircraft, delivered as RH377, and it saw virtually no active service prior to being declared surplus. It is currently in storage in Spain for eventual restoration.

Miles delivered this Messenger to Switzerland where it spent less than 12 months flying as HB-EEC. For almost 10 years it flew with Shell Mex from Elstree, but was subsequently destroyed in a fatal crash at Ashurst, West Sussex in June 1968.

Messenger G-AJDF, in front of the old terminal building at Edinburgh's Turnhouse Airport while in service with A.W. Ogston of Perth. It was the second production RAF aircraft and spent much of its time in Scotland after civilianisation. It was eventually scrapped in the late 1960s.

The external flaps of the Messenger are clearly seen in this landing shot of G-AKIN. Painted in a smart cream and red colour scheme, it has been owned by the Spiller family since July 1949 and was a regular entrant in the air competitions and races of the 1950s in the hands of A.J. Spiller.

Post-war diversification took Miles Aircraft into many new ventures outside the aviation field. In association with Mr Martin, they set up a manufacturing plant to make the Biro pen. This was the first ballpoint pen to become available and was the brainchild of Ladislao Biro, who not only devised the ballbearing writing tip but also the viscous ink which made the pen operate.

# Four

# Research and Development

The Miles brothers were restless and energetic. They recognised great opportunities for aviation and came up with innovative solutions. In the mid 1930s, F.G. Miles became interested in large long-range transport aircraft and developed concepts which continued for a number of years and culminated in the X.11 transatlantic airliner design of 1943. The 'X' designs, which were in advance of their time, were based on a fuselage with an aerofoil lifting profile and wings which were heavily contoured so as to merge into the fuselage. It was an alternative to a flying wing design and the design studies also covered proposals ranging from a heavy bomber to a version of the X.7, which could carry 550 troops in a double-deck fuselage. The many project studies led to Miles building an experimental aircraft named the X-Minor to test the 'X' concept.

Miles also experimented with the Libellula tail-first designs (commonly referred to as 'canard' designs today) for shipboard fighters, flying the M.35 and M.39 experimental research machines. Their ultimate challenge was the M.52 supersonic aircraft. This had reached an advanced stage of concept testing and a prototype was under construction when it was cancelled. The detailed design work was virtually all handed over to the Americans, substantially influencing the Bell X-1 and contributing to the subsequent American mastery of supersonic flight. Just a few of the concepts created by the Miles company are shown on the following pages.

The X-Minor, supposedly photographed in flight – but thought to be a cleverly retouched impression using a static picture of the aircraft!

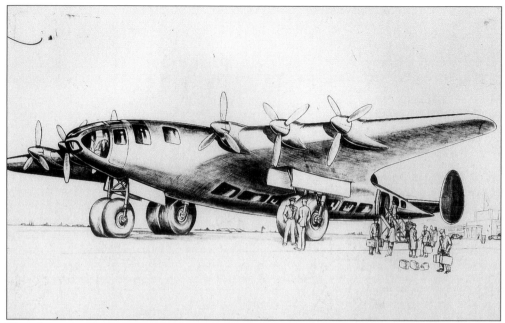

This drawing of the six-engined transatlantic X.11 project shows the highly streamlined fuselage and the smooth joining of the laminar flow wing. The main cabin windows were below wing level but there were additional skylight windows on top of the fuselage. Despite its promise, the X.11 was rejected by the Ministry of Aircraft Production as being unlikely to achieve its projected performance.

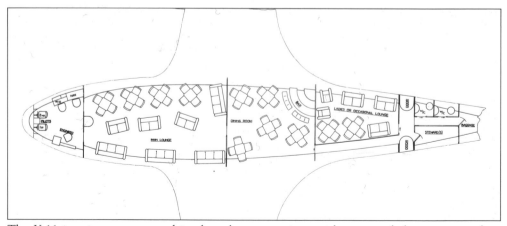

The X.11 interior was arranged in three lounge sections with two- and three-seat couches, groups of four chairs and even a bar in the corner of the central cabin. This was expected to give passengers freedom to relax on the 12 hour flight from London to New York.

To test the aerodynamic theory underlying the 'X' design, Miles built a small twin-engined test vehicle known as the M.30 X-Minor. This view shows the aerofoil shape of the fuselage. The prototype was powered by two Gipsy Major engines, which meant that the clean wing design of the full-scale 'X' airliner with engines buried in the wing could not be fully assessed.

In this picture of the X-Minor, U-0223, under construction, the complex shape of the wing root can be seen. The Miles concept was to have a wide fuselage which gradually merged into the wing structure. The X-Minor was flown by Tommy Rose in February 1942 and some useful data was gathered before the aircraft was retired to the Miles Technical School.

The problems of using conventional land-based fighters for naval carrier operations prompted George Miles to build an experimental tandem-wing aircraft named the Libellula. Constructed as a private venture in a six week period, the M.35 Libellula flew on 1 May 1942, but the Miles proposal for a full-scale shipborne fighter was turned down by the Admiralty.

George Miles is seen here landing the M.35 Libellula. It was the second Liverpool Road prototype, designated LR.2, and built without the knowledge of the Ministry – for which Miles duly received a reprimand. The first flight showed the aircraft to be unstable in pitch and, once airborne, George Miles had to use all of his skill to keep the machine flying and return for a safe landing.

Despite its lack of success as a naval fighter proposal, the M.35 had shown that a tail-first layout had many valuable characteristics. Miles envisaged a high altitude bomber to this design which would be powered by jet engines then under development. To test the theory, and on this occasion with official approval, they constructed a five-eighths flying scale model designated M.39B.

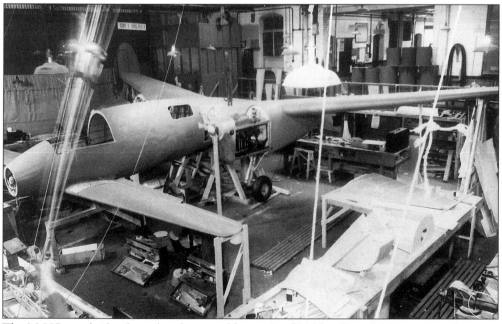

The M.39B was built of wood and powered by a pair of 140 hp Gipsy Major engines. It is seen here under construction in the spring of 1943 at the Liverpool Road factory with the port engine in the process of installation. As the third project from the experimental department, it was designated LR.3.

The M.39B Libellula was initially registered U-0244. It was flown for the first time on 22 July 1943 by George Miles and showed excellent stability and a wide centre of gravity range. The M.39B was handed over to the Royal Aircraft Establishment for testing with the serial number SR392, but later returned to Miles re-marked with the registration U4.

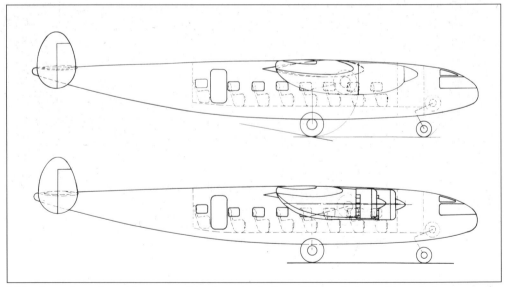

Miles investigated a wide range of projects including airliner designs. One of these was the pressurized, all-metal M.56 with 24 passenger seats and a pair of Bristol Perseus engines. The M.56A (lower view) was to be fitted with four Armstrong Siddeley Cheetapard radials. Intended as a DC-3 replacement, it was not authorised for production by the Air Ministry.

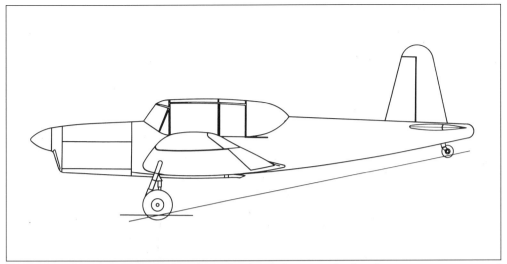

The Miles design team produced a number of proposals for low-wing training and communications aircraft. One of these was the M.53 trainer which provided side-by-side seating for the student and instructor, together with a rear seat for a second student to observe. In the event, the new trainer contract was awarded to the Percival Prentice.

In 1941, Miles developed another clandestine project known as the 'Hoopla'. This was an unmanned aircraft capable of carrying a 1,000 lb high explosive bomb beneath the fuselage. Built of wood, it was to be powered by a Cirrus Major engine and would have been an effective equivalent to the German 'doodle bug' if it had been produced in quantity.

Troop carrying gliders played an important part in the Second World War and Miles put forward its M.32 proposal for a 25-troop glider equipped with a nose ramp for loading jeeps or field guns. The M.32, which was not ordered, could be fitted with a pair of Bristol Mercury pusher engines which would make it independently powered once towed into the air.

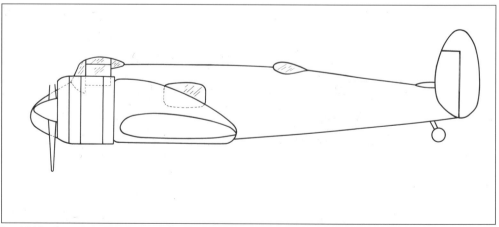

In 1942, the ever-inventive Miles team submitted the design of a small twin-engined crew trainer to the Ministry of Aircraft Production. Aimed at the training of bomber crews, the M.36 Montrose could be powered either by two Pratt & Whitney Wasps or four Armstrong Siddeley Cheetahs. As with many promising Miles projects, the Montrose was never built.

Towards the middle of the war, Miles drew up plans for various types of post-war airline aircraft to meet the specifications of the Brabazon Committee. The smallest of these was the M.51 Minerva which would carry eight passengers and followed the high wing layout which was later to be used on the Miles Marathon.

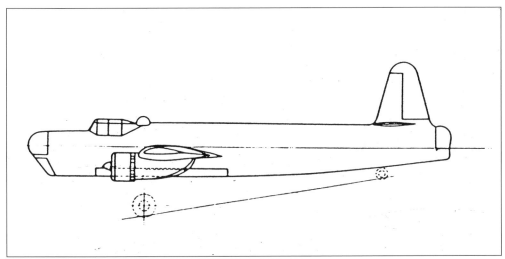

The bomber crew training requirement which had prompted the design of the Miles Montrose gave rise to a larger four-engined design, the M.55 Marlborough. Using many standard components from other Miles aircraft, the M.55 could also be used as a paratroop trainer, glider tug and minelayer. Once again, the Ministry did not proceed with the requirement.

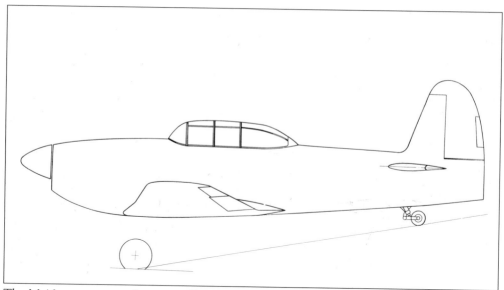

The M.46 was a proposed two-seat flying testbed for the new Rolls Royce P.I.26 supercharged diesel engine. Proposed by Miles in 1943, it would have used wings from a North American Mustang but the project did not progress beyond the design stage.

Miles established the small department at Liverpool Road in Reading where many of the experimental projects were conceived. The little M.64 LR.5 two-seat club trainer was built by the employees and flew as U-0253 on 3 June 1945. Unfortunately, it had stability problems due to fuselage design and was abandoned due to the pressure of other work at Miles.

In 1943, The Ministry of Aircraft Production awarded a contract to Miles to develop a jet aircraft which could achieve 1,000 mph in a dive. A full-size wooden mock-up of the M.52 was built with a nose mounted crew module, which could be jettisoned in an emergency, and an annular air intake behind. Construction of two prototypes was put in hand but, in February 1946, the project was suddenly cancelled.

The Miles wind tunnel at Woodley was used to test models of the M.52 and the revolutionary shape of the tail unit and wings is evident here. The design of the 'biconvex' wings was tested on the 'Gillette Falcon' (see page 40) and the work done on the M.52 up to cancellation, together with later technical assessments, showed that the aircraft would achieve the required supersonic performance.

Seen here is the Miles concept for a 'car of the air' with a detachable tail, which would then allow the main forward section to be used as a motor car. Miles did not progress beyond the concept stage but this idea was subsequently applied in other designs, notably Molt Taylor's Aerocars and the Fulton Airphibian.

Another notable example of Miles innovation was the Copycat photocopier. Using a wet process, this was was one of the earliest practical copiers and was sold in some numbers.

# Five
# Planes for Peace

With the end of the war in sight, Miles Aircraft was faced with the challenge of filling the production capacity created for wartime production with designs which could be sold to civil aircraft operators. The Messenger was already in full scale development and promised to be a popular replacement for the pre-war Falcon and Whitney Straight. Miles saw opportunities for new models ranging from light utility designs up to the airline types specified by the Brabazon Committee.

Once freed from the constraints imposed by the Ministry of Aircraft Production, Miles moved its production lines at Woodley over to building the Aerovan light freighter and the Gemini light twin, and they developed a new factory at Newtownards in Northern Ireland to handle the Messenger line. While all this activity was going on, they built prototypes of the M.68 Boxcar and M.71 Merchantman, which were outgrowths of the Aerovan design. They also made the great step into all-metal construction with the Marathon local service airliner, which flew in prototype form early in 1946.

Such a range of new projects put great strain on the company. The financial demands and learning curves of so many new models, together with the hard winter of 1947, proved too much for Miles. A Receiver was appointed and only the Marathon survived the period – with Handley Page who took over the Woodley aircraft production facilities. George Miles went to work for Airspeed and F.G. Miles established himself at Redhill and later at Shoreham and played an important part in the creation of Beagle Aircraft.

The Aerovan was a highly innovative post-war design devised by George Miles and the prototype is seen here during test flights over Woodley. It was the fourth of the Liverpool Road prototypes. For some unexplained reason the Aerovan prototype was painted with RAF roundels and tail stripes.

The first Aerovan made its maiden flight on 26 January 1945 and is seen here at a snowy Woodley Aerodrome before being painted in its final silver colour scheme. The prototype had rectangular cabin windows, but production Aerovans had round portholes and a longer fuselage.

Production of the all-wood Aerovans is seen here in full swing, with work being carried out on the installation of the port engine of the leading aircraft. Five Aerovans are shown in final assembly and a batch of 50 aircraft was completed by the time the line closed in early 1948.

Another snowy day at Woodley found the Aerovan sales demonstrator, G-AILF, equipped with skis. Seen here taxying out for take off, this aircraft was completed in October 1946 and was later sold to the haulage and removals company, Pickfords. It was eventually destroyed in a landing accident at Guernsey in August 1950.

In the development of the Aerovan concept, Miles studied several variations. One of these was a flying boat version with a boat hull, which might have gone into production if the company had survived a little longer. Visible in this artist's impression are the retractable stabilisers fitted to the fuselage.

With Woodley operating at full capacity, it was arranged that the factory at Newtownards in Northern Ireland would help the production effort by building mainspars for the Miles Gemini. The problem of transporting these completed spars was solved by using the prototype Aerovan, with suitable modifications, and the aircraft is shown here being unloaded.

The M.57 Aerovan prototype with a pair of Gemini spars installed in the main cabin. A gap in the rear loading doors allowed the full length of the spars to be accommodated and an additional supporting strap was fitted to the tailboom.

The Royal New Zealand Air Force used the last production Aerovan for a while as NZ1751 for agricultural top dressing experiments. It was returned to the civil register as ZK-AWV and was destroyed in November 1951, while landing in strong winds at Rongotai.

Another view of the first M.57 at Woodley shows the aircraft being inspected by a foreign military delegation. The rear loading door can be clearly seen in the open position. In the background is a line-up of RAF Tiger Moths and several Magisters and Masters. A solitary Spitfire is a reminder of the large overhaul operation set up by Miles to restore war-weary and damaged fighters at Woodley.

Aerovan G-AILM was used by Space Neon as a platform for aerial advertising with a large neon tube display fixed to the fuselage sides. The illuminated lettering of the company's name can be seen in this picture, which also shows the additional framework fixed beneath the tailboom to support the large tube structure.

One Aerovan, G-AKHF, was converted as the sole Aerovan VI with a pair of 195 hp Lycoming O-435-A engines and deeper endplate fins. This Aerovan, seen here in 1949 landing on Runway 01 at Redhill, was sold in 1954 to Italy as I-VALK. Hangar 8, which was used by Miles at Redhill and is still operated by Acebell Aviation, is visible in the background.

Seen here at Le Bourget in July 1953, F-BFPF started its career with Ulster Aviation in Northern Ireland and operated freight services to Croydon and elsewhere. The large Aerovan's crew entrance door is well illustrated.

One interesting Aerovan development was the HDM.105, which flew on 31 March 1957 and is seen here with the 'B' markings G-35-3. It was an existing Aerovan, G-AJOF, fitted by Miles with a very high aspect ratio wing based on principles established by the French company, Hurel Dubois, so as to carry out comparison tests with the earlier HD.31 and the HD.32 aerial mapping aircraft.

The HDM.105, probably at Paris, in front of a line of Dassault Mysteres, was re-registered G-AHDM and appeared at the Farnborough Air Show in September 1957. Its career was relatively short and it was destroyed in June of the following year, when the tailboom collapsed during a landing at Shoreham. The HDM.105 design led to George Miles' HDM.106 Caravan, which was developed into the Short Skyvan.

George Miles decided that the Aerovan concept offered many possibilities, one of which was as a container carrier. Miles Aircraft built a prototype of the M.68 Boxcar, which could be fitted with a removable freight container fitted under the centre fuselage. Registered G-AJJM, the M.68 flew in August 1947 and is seen here with a container full of Biro pens!

Another variant on the Aerovan theme was the M.71 Merchantman developed to the order of Air Contractors Ltd. In fact, this was virtually a new design and was of all-metal construction with four 250 hp Gipsy Queen 30 in-line engines. The Merchantman was initially designed as a flying horsebox, but it could handle a wide variety of freight with loading via a large rear door.

The Merchantman, seen here with its test registration, U-21 made its first flight at Woodley on 7 August 1947. The wing and engine installation was very similar to that of the Miles Marathon which was then under development. The Merchantman was abandoned when the financial collapse occurred at Miles Aircraft.

With the Messenger established in production, Miles decided to produce a light twin-engined aircraft based on the M.38 airframe. The prototype M.65 Gemini, G-AGUS, made its maiden flight on 26 October 1945, powered by a pair of 100 hp Cirrus Minor engines. In this picture of the prototype, the square rear windows, unique to this aircraft, can be seen.

The Gemini prototype was subsequently converted as the sole Gemini 2 with two Continental C-125-2 flat-four engines which were readily identified by their prominent exhaust stacks. In this picture of G-AGUS, the large twin fins which replaced the triple tail of the Messenger are well illustrated, as is the retractable tailwheel undercarriage.

The Gemini was successful not only with British customers but also in export markets. One of the more unusual overseas deliveries was YI-ABC, delivered to Iraq. Here the external trailing edge flaps are clearly visible. Production Geminis also had lozenge-shaped rear windows instead of the square windows of the prototype.

Gemini 1A, G-AJZO, was a resident of Elstree Aerodrome and is seen here parked at the airfield in September 1966. This picture clearly shows the upward opening main cabin doors fitted to the Gemini. G-AJZO was owned by the brewing company, Whitbreads, for many years and was eventually retired from service in 1973.

One of the early Gemini exports was G-AILK, which was sold to Australia. It was flown on its delivery flight, at the end of 1946, by Group Captain A.F. 'Bush' Bandidt and was then re-registered VH-BJZ. It continued in service until March 1963.

The Gemini Mk. 3A was a much improved version, with 145 hp Gipsy Major 10 engines replacing the 100 hp Cirrus Minors on the Mk.1A. Six were produced in 1950, by Wolverhampton Aviation, from uncompleted Woodley-built airframes. G-AKEK was converted from a Gemini 1A and in this picture, taken amidst the buttercups at Biggin Hill, the deeper nacelles of the larger powerplants are readily identifiable.

The Gemini 1A, G-AJZK, at Woodley in the summer of 1947, shortly after being handed over to the Missionary Aviation Fellowship. It departed for Africa under the banner of *The Missionary Pathfinder*. Regrettably, its religious task was cut short a year later when it crashed in the Belgian Congo.

G-AKKH is one of the longer-surviving Geminis – seen here flying over White Waltham in the mid-1980s. Owned for many years by S. Bourne & Co., it was intended for export to the Belgian Congo, but this deal collapsed. It is now owned by Mike Russell, although it has been in storage since 1996.

Gemini G-AIDO became the only three-engined Miles aircraft when it was fitted with a mock-up of an engine nacelle in the nose. This nacelle followed the same contours as a standard Gipsy Major installation and was used for investigation into wing root stall problems which were affecting the Messenger.

One of the most famous Geminis was the bronze-painted G-ALZG of Percy Blamire, which was a frequent participant in the air races of the 1950s and 1960s. It was subsequently sold to Ireland and is seen here at Redhill with its Irish registration, E1-BHJ, showing its age with a somewhat wrinkled plywood covering to its rear fuselage.

This interesting picture of a low loader taken, at the Miles factory, shows an export Gemini, thought to be ZK-AUA for New Zealand, in dismantled condition on its wooden shipping pallet. Apparently, the rear fuselage was detachable at a point just behind the wing root.

After the collapse of Miles Aircraft, F.G. Miles moved to Redhill and restarted operations in December 1948, in a much more modest fashion. One of the first projects was an improvement to the Gemini, involving the fitment of 155 hp Cirrus Major III engines. The M.75 Aries prototype, G-35-1, is seen here with the larger fins which were necessary to handle the increased power.

Only two examples of the M.75 Aries were completed from Woodley-built components, although two other Gemini 3As were modified to this standard with 155 hp Cirrus Major III engines. The second machine, G-AOGA, is seen here at White Waltham, showing the enlarged air intakes for the new nacelles. This Aries spent some time with an owner in Ireland and was finally retired from service in 1984.

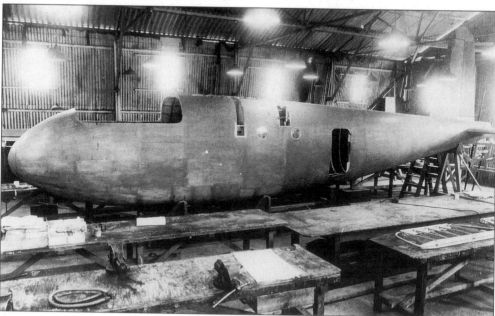

An important aspect of Miles operations was the Technical Training School, which was established at Davis Farm, near Woodley Aerodrome, with the particular backing of Blossom Miles. The students constructed the fuselage of the TS Venture – a twin-engined aircraft intended as a testbed for Miles lightweight autopilots, but the project was not completed beyond the stage seen here.

The major post-war project for Miles was the M.60 Marathon - a 14-passenger feeder liner powered by four Gipsy Queen 71 engines. The second prototype, G-AILH, seen here, shows the twin fin arrangement which was tested at an early stage. The production Marathon was fitted with three fins. The Marathon prototype, marked U10, was first flown on 19 May 1946 by Ken Waller.

The Marathon was the first all-metal aircraft built by Miles and two prototypes were built by the company, followed by forty constructed by Handley Page after the Miles collapse. A BEA order for twenty-five was anticipated, but when this failed to materialise, 27 completed Marathons were delivered to the RAF as navigation trainers, one of which was XA260 shown here.

The main British civilian operator of the Marathon was Derby Airways which had three examples, based at Derby's Burnaston airfield. G-AMEW, seen here at Turnhouse fitted with twenty passenger seats, was a former RAF aircraft and was finally retired in 1962. Sister ships G-AMGW and G-AMHR were scrapped at Burnaston in December 1960.

The twelfth production Marathon, G-AMEO, was used as a demonstrator for West African Airways Corporation during 1951 and is seen here in WAAC livery, prior to departure. It later returned to be sold to the German airways radio calibration unit based at Frankfurt and was eventually withdrawn from use in January 1962.

One of the early RAF Marathons to be delivered was XA254, which served with No. 2 Air Navigation School at Thorney Island. On 9 January 1956 it skidded off a wet runway while landing, destroying both itself and a parked vehicle in the process.

The third prototype Marathon was eventually completed in 1949, after the financial crisis hit Miles. It became the M.69 Marathon II, fitted with two Armstrong Siddeley Mamba turboprop engines, and was first flown by Hugh Kendall as G-AHXU on 23 July 1949. The aircraft was subsequently fitted with Alvis Leonides engines as part of the Herald development.

While at Redhill, F.G. Miles developed a jet-powered modification of a Miles Sparrowhawk for racing pilot Fred Dunkerley. The M.77 Sparrowjet, which was completed at Shoreham, had two Turbomeca Palas jets in the wing roots and is seen here as G-ADNL on the occasion of its winning the 1957 King's Cup at Coventry.

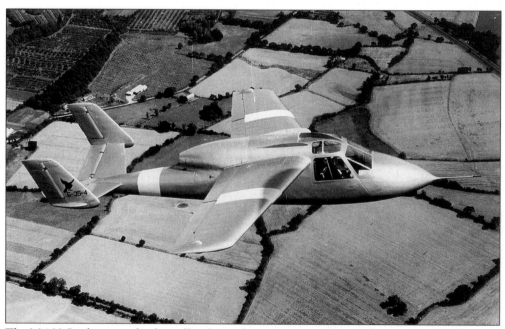

The M.100 Student was the first official new design project of the newly constituted F.G. Miles Ltd, which was established at Shoreham in 1953. It was an all-metal jet trainer aimed at providing a low cost replacement for the Percival Provost piston-engined trainers then in service. Here, the prototype is seen over Sussex with initial test markings, G-35-4.

The Student had side-by-side seating for instructor and student and was powered by a single Blackburn Turbomeca Marboré turbojet, mounted above and behind the wing with a large NACA tapered intake positioned above the cabin. In this picture of the Student in landing configuration, it carries the civil registration G-APLK.

After Miles moved from Shoreham to Ford, the Student prototype was converted to Student II status with a Marboré 6F engine. It later passed to Aces High, being re-registered G-MIOO, but was substantially damaged following engine failure on take-off from Duxford on 24 August 1985. The Museum of Berkshire Aviation at Woodley now has the remains for a rebuild to static display condition.

The acquisition of F.G. Miles by Beagle brought with it the design of a light twin, known as the M.115. This was a George Miles design and was eventually built as the Beagle M.218 – the last true Miles design to take to the air. This sole prototype, G-ASCK, which later formed the basis for the Beagle 242, is seen here over Shoreham with the port engine feathered.

After moving to Ford, George Miles pursued various engineering projects, including the Centurion business jet based on the Student. In this 1960s view, George Miles is on the left and 'F.G.' is on the right in front of the Centurion mock-up.